The children put on a circus.

Kipper was a clown.

Floppy pulled his leg.

Chip was a strong-man.

He made everyone laugh.

Wilma and Biff did gymnastics.

The
Jumping
Beans
(Biff and Wilma)
Amazing
Gymnasts

Everyone had a drink.

"What a good circus!"
said Mum.

Wilf was a stuntman.

Kipper was fed up.

He wanted to be a stuntman.

“Look at me!” he said.

Everyone looked at Kipper.

Oh no!

"I'm a clown, after all,"
said Kipper.